MY FIRST

Poem

Cambridgeshire & Suffolk

Edited By Jenni Harrison

First published in Great Britain in 2017 by:

Young Writers
Remus House
Coltsfoot Drive
Peterborough
PE2 9BF
Telephone: 01733 890066
Website: www.youngwriters.co.uk

Foreword

Young Writers was established in 1991 with the aim of
encouraging writing skills in young people and giving
them the opportunity to see their work in print. Poetry is a
wonderful way to introduce young children to the idea of
rhyme and rhythm and helps learning and development
of communication, language and literacy skills.
'My First Poem' was created to introduce nursery and
preschool children to this wonderful world of poetry.
They were given a template to fill in with their own words,
creating a poem that was all about them.
We are proud to present the resulting collection
of personal and touching poems in this anthology,
which can be treasured for years to come.

Jenni Bannister

Editorial Manager

Contents

Bright Stars Day Nursery, Peterborough

Tiana Bhambra-Celaire (2)	1
Connor Rutledge (3)	2
James Eckardt (3)	3
Sami Tye (2)	4
Evelyn McPherson	5
Aisha Malik (3)	6
Jack Norbury (3)	7

Chelmondiston Playgroup, Ipswich

Alfie Arnold (4)	8
Oliver Parish (4)	9
Timothy John Roberts (2)	10
Chloe Eve Hill (3)	11
Grace Warner (3)	12
Hugo Ellis Bergdahl (4)	13
Jack Nunn (2)	14
Harriet Welham (2)	15
Isla Mae Reeveley (4)	16
Amelia Gorman (3)	17

Felixstowe Opportunity Group, Felixstowe

Cleo Woodhouse (3)	18
Riley Ellis (4)	19
Josie Carbin (3)	20
Bradley Carbin (3)	21
Roman Shaw Duff (2)	22
Lucas Battle (3)	23
Liam Dunmore (3)	24

Patacake Day Nursery, Cambridge

Joshua Henry Lees (4)	25
Anati Ludidi (4)	26
Alexander Lynn (3)	27
Olive Johnson (4)	28
Sophia Coppola (4)	29
Austin Zhang (4)	30
Tabitha Sanders (3)	31
George Fishlock (4)	32
Robin Holborow (4)	33
Liam Mouchliantis (3)	34
Theo Stephens-Uddin (3)	35
Yani Nemiri (3)	36
Martha Nitch-Smith (3)	37
Axa Dragojevic (3)	38
Flynn Holborow (4)	39
Ada Horsnel (4)	40
Ezgi Kaser (4)	41
Finn Baker-Cash (4)	42
Maisy Campbell (3)	43
Samuel Ray (3)	44

Playtimes Preschool, Huntingdon

Amelia-Grace Godden (2)	45
George Howell-Jones (2)	46
Lily Woods (3)	47
Maisie Woods (3)	48

Rainbow Bright Private Day Care, Ipswich

Poppy Watson (4)	49
Kyle Rogers (4)	50
Isabel Hatchard (3)	51
Jasmine Watson (4)	52
Freya Souter (3)	53
Gracie Boyd (2)	54
Suzie White (2)	55
Hugo French (3)	56
Harris Scott (3)	57

Rosehill Playgroup, Ipswich

Alexis Bloomfield (4)	58
Jenna Foulkes (3)	59
Holly Pearson (3)	60
Saffire Marshall (4)	61
Rosie Adams (4)	62
Jaycie-Lee Rose Rush (3)	63
Ruby Bown (4)	64
Charlie Hazell (3)	65
Hannah Martina Walker (4)	66
Lewis Rosher (3)	67
Sonny Webb (4)	68
Blake Creasey (4)	69
Safwan Bin Subhan-Miah (4)	70
Violet Jean Richardson (3)	71

Stepping Stones Preschool, Newmarket

Lily-May Bell (4)	72
Dexter Pidsley-Cook (3)	73
Dougie Bear Mclean (2)	74
Jacob Kirby (4)	75
Kodi Lockwood (3)	76
Ellis Jeffery (3)	77
Ryan William Brewer (4)	78
Annabella Marie Rodman (3)	79

Drayton Hayes (2)	80
Thurloe Hayes (4)	81
Ben Shevki (4)	82
Henry Thomas Palmer (2)	83
Rosie O'Brien (3)	84
Florrie Shaw (3)	85
Iyla Frankie Jack (3)	86

Sunflower Nursery, Cambridge

Rowan Kearney (4)	87
Lingwen Linus Chin (4)	88
Thom Blanchard (4)	89
Leila Daisy Fievet (3)	90
Henry Heywood (4)	91
Margaret Zi Yin Li (3)	92
Maria Popescu (4)	93
Georgie-Rose Jeffrey (3)	94
Nicholas Jameson (3)	95
Beatrice Raine (4)	96
Kate Bleazard (4)	97
Jasper Giles (4)	98
Lawrence Heywood (4)	99
Ivan Kolesnik (4)	100
Kasey Kwateng (4)	101
Rosie-May Anne Abbs (4)	102
Holly York (4)	103
Anamaya Rose Kumar (3)	104

Trinity Nursery, Lowestoft

Erin Howes (2)	105
Brody Baxter (3)	106
Emily Pearl Newton (3)	107
Mia-Rose Woodard (4)	108
Archie Theobald (3)	109
Ivy Grace Harrison (3)	110
Ethan Howes (3)	111
Jack Graham (3)	112
Christopher-Junior Jayden Spencer (3)	113

The Poems

Tiana's First Poem

My name is Tiana and I go to preschool,

My best friends are Ava-Mae and Aisha, who are really cool.

I watch Peppa Pig on TV,

Playing with Joell, Mummy and Nanny is lots of fun for me.

I just love custard to eat,

And sometimes banana for a treat.

Black is a colour I like a lot,

My mummy is the best present I ever got.

My favourite people are Mummy and Joell and Nanny, who are gems,

So this, my first poem, is just for them!

Tiana Bhambra-Celaire (2)
Bright Stars Day Nursery, Peterborough

Connor's First Poem

My name is Connor and I go to preschool,

My best friend is Mummy, who is really cool.

I watch PAW Patrol on TV,

Playing with construction straws is lots of fun for me.

I just love sandwiches to eat,

And sometimes hot cross buns for a treat.

Pink is a colour I like a lot,

My train carriage is the best present I ever got.

My favourite person is Daddy, who is a gem,

So this, my first poem, is just for them!

Connor Rutledge (3)

Bright Stars Day Nursery, Peterborough

James' First Poem

My name is James and I go to preschool,

My best friend is Mummy, who is really cool.

I watch PAW Patrol on TV,

Playing with the garbage truck is lots of fun

for me.

I just love spaghetti to eat,

And sometimes jelly beans for a treat.

Yellow is a colour I like a lot,

My truck is the best present I ever got.

My favourite person is Daddy, who is a gem,

So this, my first poem, is just for them!

James Eckardt (3)

Bright Stars Day Nursery, Peterborough

Sami's First Poem

My name is Sami and I go to preschool,
My best friend is Mummy, who is really cool.
I watch Choo Choo on TV,
Playing with animals is lots of fun for me.
I just love choc choc eggy to eat,
And sometimes more for a treat.
Orange is a colour I like a lot,
My choo-choo is the best present I ever got.
My favourite person is Mummy, who is a gem,
So this, my first poem, is just for them!

Sami Tye (2)

Bright Stars Day Nursery, Peterborough

Evelyn's First Poem

My name is Evelyn and I go to preschool,

My best friend is Isabelle, who is really cool.

I watch CBeebies on TV,

Playing a trumpet is lots of fun for me.

I just love pasta to eat,

And sometimes chocolate for a treat.

Pink is a colour I like a lot,

My train track is the best present I ever got.

My favourite person is Mummy, who is a gem,

So this, my first poem, is just for them!

Evelyn McPherson
Bright Stars Day Nursery, Peterborough

Aisha's First Poem

My name is Aisha and I go to preschool,
My best friend is Jack, who is really cool.
I watch Peter Rabbit on TV,
Playing Gummy Bears is lots of fun for me.
I just love banana to eat,
And sometimes potatoes for a treat.
Green is a colour I like a lot,
My Mia doll is the best present I ever got.
My favourite person is Mummy, who is a gem,
So this, my first poem, is just for them!

Aisha Malik (3)

Bright Stars Day Nursery, Peterborough

Jack's First Poem

My name is Jack and I go to preschool,

My best friend is Megan, who is really cool.

I watch PAW Patrol on TV,

Playing with Lesley is lots of fun for me.

I just love sandwiches to eat,

And sometimes a picnic for a treat.

Red is a colour I like a lot,

My lorry is the best present I ever got.

My favourite person is Mummy, who is a gem,

So this, my first poem, is just for them!

Jack Norbury (3)

Bright Stars Day Nursery, Peterborough

Alfie's First Poem

My name is Alfie and I go to preschool,

My best friend is Mummy, who is really cool.

I watch PAW Patrol on TV,

Playing with my cars is lots of fun for me.

I just love pizza to eat,

And sometimes sweeties for a treat.

Blue is a colour I like a lot,

My Rescue Bot is the best present I ever got.

My favourite person is Daddy, who is a gem,

So this, my first poem, is just for them!

Alfie Arnold (4)

Chelmondiston Playgroup, Ipswich

Oliver's First Poem

My name is Oliver and I go to preschool,

My best friend is Tori, who is really cool.

I watch PAW Patrol on TV,

Playing hide and seek is lots of fun for me.

I just love spaghetti Bolognese to eat,

And sometimes rice pudding for a treat.

Red is a colour I like a lot,

My big Jupiter is the best present I ever got.

My favourite person is Chloe, who is a gem,

So this, my first poem, is just for them!

Oliver Parish (4)

Chelmondiston Playgroup, Ipswich

Timothy's First Poem

My name is Timothy and I go to preschool,

My best friend is Isaac, who is really cool.

I watch Peppa Pig (oink!) on TV,

Playing policemen is lots of fun for me.

I just love carrots to eat,

And sometimes sweets for a treat.

Yellow is a colour I like a lot,

My policeman hat is the best present I ever got.

My favourite person is Mummy, who is a gem,

So this, my first poem, is just for them!

Timothy John Roberts (2)

Chelmondiston Playgroup, Ipswich

Chloe's First Poem

My name is Chloe and I go to preschool,

My best friend is Austin, who is really cool.

I watch Trolls on TV,

Playing in the mud kitchen is lots of fun for me.

I just love tomato soup to eat,

And sometimes sweets for a treat.

Pink is a colour I like a lot,

My Honey Bees game is the best present I ever got.

My favourite person is Kelly, who is a gem,

So this, my first poem, is just for them!

Chloe Eve Hill (3)

Chelmondiston Playgroup, Ipswich

Grace's First Poem

My name is Grace and I go to preschool,
My best friend is Audrey, who is really cool.
I watch Peppa Pig on TV,
Playing with babies is lots of fun for me.
I just love meatballs and pasta to eat,
And sometimes chocolate for a treat.
Blue is a colour I like a lot,
My car is the best present I ever got.
My favourite person is Bobby, who is a gem,
So this, my first poem, is just for them!

Grace Warner (3)
Chelmondiston Playgroup, Ipswich

Hugo's First Poem

My name is Hugo and I go to preschool,

My best friend is Oliver, who is really cool.

I watch PAW Patrol on TV,

Playing chase outside is lots of fun for me.

I just love pasta to eat,

And sometimes McDonald's for a treat.

Blue is a colour I like a lot,

My Pikachu is the best present I ever got.

My favourite person is Kestra, who is a gem,

So this, my first poem, is just for them!

Hugo Ellis Bergdahl (4)

Chelmondiston Playgroup, Ipswich

Jack's First Poem

My name is Jack and I go to preschool,

My best friend is Mummy, who is really cool.

I watch football on TV,

Playing with my tractors is lots of fun for me.

I just love chicken to eat,

And sometimes cake for a treat.

Purple is a colour I like a lot,

My kitchen is the best present I ever got.

My favourite person is Daddy, who is a gem,

So this, my first poem, is just for them!

Jack Nunn (2)

Chelmondiston Playgroup, Ipswich

Harriet's First Poem

My name is Harriet and I go to preschool,

My best friend is Amber, who is really cool.

I watch Peppa Pig on TV,

Playing babies is lots of fun for me.

I just love jam to eat,

And sometimes a lollipop for a treat.

Pink is a colour I like a lot,

My Peppa Pig is the best present I ever got.

My favourite person is Mummy, who is a gem,

So this, my first poem, is just for them!

Harriet Welham (2)

Chelmondiston Playgroup, Ipswich

Isla's First Poem

My name is Isla and I go to preschool,

My best friend is Molly, who is really cool.

I watch Peppa Pig on TV,

Playing with animals is lots of fun for me.

I just love grapes to eat,

And sometimes sweets for a treat.

Red is a colour I like a lot,

My babies are the best present I ever got.

My favourite person is Mummy, who is a gem,

So this, my first poem, is just for them!

Isla Mae Reeveley (4)

Chelmondiston Playgroup, Ipswich

Amelia's First Poem

My name is Amelia and I go to preschool,
My best friend is Sam, who is really cool.
I watch Peppa Pig on TV,
Playing with puzzles is lots of fun for me.
I just love chips to eat,
And sometimes cake for a treat.
Pink is a colour I like a lot,
My Batgirl is the best present I ever got.
My favourite person is Mummy, who is a gem,
So this, my first poem, is just for them!

Amelia Gorman (3)

Chelmondiston Playgroup, Ipswich

Cleo's First Poem

My name is Cleo and I go to preschool,

My best friend is Noah, who is really cool.

I watch Noddy and Mickey Mouse Clubhouse on TV,

Playing with Play-Doh and my dog is lots of fun for me.

I just love fish fingers and popcorn to eat,

And sometimes flapjacks and pizza for a treat.

Blue is a colour I like a lot,

My bus is the best present I ever got.

My favourite person is Noah, who is a gem,

So this, my first poem, is just for them!

Cleo Woodhouse (3)
Felixstowe Opportunity Group, Felixstowe

Riley's First Poem

My name is Riley and I go to preschool,

My best friend is Bradley, who is really cool.

I watch PAW Patrol, Blaze and the Monster Machines on TV,

Playing with my PAW Patrol Look-out Tower is lots of fun for me.

I just love raspberries to eat,

And sometimes Kinder Eggs for a treat.

Blue is a colour I like a lot,

My big digger is the best present I ever got.

My favourite person is Nanny, who is a gem,

So this, my first poem, is just for them!

Riley Ellis (4)

Felixstowe Opportunity Group, Felixstowe

Josie's First Poem

My name is Josie and I go to preschool,

My best friend is my big sister, Molly, who is

really cool.

I watch PAW Patrol and Peppa Pig on TV,

Playing cooking in the kitchen is lots of fun for me.

I just love sausages to eat,

And sometimes ice cream for a treat.

Pink is a colour I like a lot,

My chocolate is the best present I ever got.

My favourite people are my family, who are all gems,

So this, my first poem, is just for them!

Josie Carbin (3)

Felixstowe Opportunity Group, Felixstowe

Bradley's First Poem

My name is Bradley and I go to preschool,

My best friend is Freddie, who is really cool.

I watch Peppa Pig, Blaze and PAW Patrol

on TV,

Playing with bin lorries is lots of fun for me.

I just love sausages to eat,

And sometimes pancakes for a treat.

Red is a colour I like a lot,

My bin lorry is the best present I ever got.

My favourite person is Max, the dog, who is a gem,

So this, my first poem, is just for them!

Bradley Carbin (3)

Felixstowe Opportunity Group, Felixstowe

Roman's First Poem

My name is Roman and I go to preschool,
My best friend is Riley, who is really cool.
I watch Topsy and Tim on TV,
Playing with trains is lots of fun for me.
I just love jam on toast to eat,
And sometimes an ice cream for a treat.
Yellow is a colour I like a lot,
My play kitchen is the best present I ever got.
My favourite person is my brother, Kian, who is
a gem,
So this, my first poem, is just for them!

Roman Shaw Duff (2)
Felixstowe Opportunity Group, Felixstowe

Lucas' First Poem

My name is Lucas and I go to preschool,
My best friend is Kaden, who is really cool.
I watch Bing Bunny on TV,
Playing on my keyboard is lots of fun for me.
I just love sausages and cake to eat,
And sometimes profiteroles for a treat.
Blue is a colour I like a lot,
My Thomas the Tank Engine book is the best
present I ever got.
My favourite person is Oma, who is a gem,
So this, my first poem, is just for them!

Lucas Battle (3)

Felixstowe Opportunity Group, Felixstowe

Liam's First Poem

My name is **Liam** and I go to preschool,
My best friend is **Mummy**, who is really cool.
I watch **Team Umizoomi** on TV,
Playing **trains** is lots of fun for me.
I just love **cucumber, cheese and ham** to eat,
And sometimes **sweeties** for a treat.
Red and green are colours I like a lot,
My **green train** is the best present I ever got.
My favourite person is **Jacob**, who is a gem,
So this, my first poem, is just for them!

Liam Dunmore (3)
Felixstowe Opportunity Group, Felixstowe

Joshua's First Poem

My name is Joshua and I go to preschool,
My best friends are Betty and Olive, who are
really cool.
I watch Toy Story on TV,
Playing subway surface is lots of fun for me.
I just love Daddy's pasta to eat,
And sometimes some chocolate orange
cheesecake for a treat.
Dark green is a colour I like a lot,
My Playmobil rocket is the best present I ever got.
My favourite animal is my cat, Millie, who is a gem,
So this, my first poem, is just for them!

Joshua Henry Lees (4)
Patacake Day Nursery, Cambridge

Anati's First Poem

My name is **Anati** and I go to preschool,

My best friends are **Yugiao, Joshua and Olive**, who are really cool.

I watch **Dr McStuffins** on TV,

Playing **doctors and hospitals** is lots of fun for me.

I just love **fish fingers and chips** to eat,

And sometimes **ice cream** for a treat.

Orange is a colour I like a lot,

My **My Little Pony** is the best present I ever got.

My favourite person is **Nina, my sister**, who is a gem,

So this, my first poem, is just for them!

Anati Ludidi (4)

Patacake Day Nursery, Cambridge

Alexander's First Poem

My name is Alexander and I go to preschool,
I'm best friends with everybody, they are
really cool.
I watch Octonauts on TV,
Playing Mega Bloks is lots of fun for me.
I just love potatoes to eat,
And sometimes chocolate for a treat.
I love all the colours in the rainbow a lot,
My sticky slug is the best present I ever got.
My favourite person is John, who is a gem,
So this, my first poem, is just for them!

Alexander Lynn (3)

Patacake Day Nursery, Cambridge

Olive's First Poem

My name is Olive and I go to preschool,

My best friend is Romilly, who is really cool.

I watch 101 Dalmatians on TV,

Playing mums and dads is lots of fun for me.

I just love pasta and red sauce to eat,

And sometimes chocolate for a treat.

Pink, purple and orange are colours I like a lot,

My lion is the best present I ever got.

My favourite person is Grandad, who is a gem,

So this, my first poem, is just for them!

Olive Johnson (4)

Patacake Day Nursery, Cambridge

Sophia's First Poem

My name is Sophia and I go to preschool,

My best friends are Isabella and Carla, who

are really cool.

I watch Peppa Pig on TV,

Playing games with my mummy is lots of fun

for me.

I just love spaghetti to eat,

And sometimes chocolate eggs for a treat.

Pink is a colour I like a lot,

My doll's house is the best present I ever got.

My favourite person is Mummy, who is a gem,

So this, my first poem, is just for them!

Sophia Coppola (4)

Patacake Day Nursery, Cambridge

Austin's First Poem

My name is **Austin** and I go to preschool,
My best friend is **Zachary**, who is really cool.
I watch **Thomas the train** on TV,
Playing **with Zachary** is lots of fun for me.
I just love **fish** to eat,
And sometimes **lots of chocolate** for a treat.
Brown and black are colours I like a lot,
My **remote control aeroplane** is the best present
I ever got.
My favourite person is **Zachary**, who is a gem,
So this, my first poem, is just for them!

Austin Zhang (4)

Patacake Day Nursery, Cambridge

Tabitha's First Poem

My name is Tabitha and I go to preschool,

My best friend is Florence, who is really cool.

I watch Frozen on TV,

Playing with Elsa and Anna is lots of fun for me.

I just love sausages to eat,

And sometimes malt loaf for a treat.

Pink is a colour I like a lot,

My My Little Pony is the best present I ever got.

My favourite people are Mummy, Daddy and Jonty, who are gems,

So this, my first poem, is just for them!

Tabitha Sanders (3)

Patacake Day Nursery, Cambridge

George's First Poem

My name is George and I go to preschool,

My best friends are Aidan and Brodie, who are

really cool.

I watch PAW Patrol on TV,

Playing dinosaurs is lots of fun for me.

I just love baked beans to eat,

And sometimes pizza for a treat.

Blue is a colour I like a lot,

My Chase the dog is the best present I ever got.

I love everyone, they are all gems,

So this, my first poem, is just for them!

George Fishlock (4)

Patacake Day Nursery, Cambridge

Robin's First Poem

My name is Robin and I go to preschool,

My best friend is Carla, who is really cool.

I watch Peppa Pig on TV,

Playing with my brown puppy is lots of fun for me.

I just love spaghetti to eat,

And sometimes Haribo for a treat.

Purple is a colour I like a lot,

My talking PAW Patrol is the best present I

ever got.

My favourite person is Flynn, who is a gem,

So this, my first poem, is just for them!

Robin Holborow (4)

Patacake Day Nursery, Cambridge

Liam's First Poem

My name is Liam and I go to preschool,

My best friend is Eli, who is really cool.

I watch Star Wars on TV,

Playing with lightsabers is lots of fun for me.

I just love spaghetti to eat,

And sometimes candy for a treat.

Rainbow colours I like a lot,

My Peppa Pig camera is the best present I ever got.

My favourite people are Mummy and Daddy, who
are gems,

So this, my first poem, is just for them!

Liam Mouchliantis (3)

Patacake Day Nursery, Cambridge

Theo's First Poem

My name is Theo and I go to preschool,

My best friend is Zachary, who is really cool.

I watch Fireman Sam on TV,

Playing fire engines is lots of fun for me.

I just love banana cake to eat,

And sometimes chocolate for a treat.

Orange is a colour I like a lot,

My Fireman Sam helmet is the best present I

ever got.

My favourite person is Emilie, who is a gem,

So this, my first poem, is just for them!

Theo Stephens-Uddin (3)

Patacake Day Nursery, Cambridge

Yani's First Poem

My name is Yani and I go to preschool,

My best friend is Freddy, who is really cool.

I watch Power Rangers on TV,

Playing hide-and-seek is lots of fun for me.

I just love chips to eat,

And sometimes biscuits for a treat.

Red is a colour I like a lot,

My dinosaur is the best present I ever got.

My favourite people are my daddy and mummy,

who are gems,

So this, my first poem, is just for them!

Yani Nemiri (3)

Patacake Day Nursery, Cambridge

Martha's First Poem

My name is Martha and I go to preschool,

My best friend is Olive, who is really cool.

I watch Peppa Pig on TV,

Playing mums and dads is lots of fun for me.

I just love fish fingers and chips to eat,

And sometimes ice cream for a treat.

Pink is a colour I like a lot,

My skipping rope is the best present I ever got.

My favourite person is Esme, who is a gem,

So this, my first poem, is just for them!

Martha Nitch-Smith (3)

Patacake Day Nursery, Cambridge

Axa's First Poem

My name is Axa and I go to preschool,
My best friend is Maisy, who is really cool.
I watch PAW Patrol on TV,
Playing my cupcake game is lots of fun for me.
I just love spaghetti to eat,
And sometimes a lollipop for a treat.
Orange is a colour I like a lot,
My pink trousers are the best present I ever got.
My favourite person is my daddy, who is a gem,
So this, my first poem, is just for them!

Axa Dragojevic (3)

Patacake Day Nursery, Cambridge

Flynn's First Poem

My name is Flynn and I go to preschool,

My best friend is Clare, who is really cool.

I watch Peter Rabbit on TV,

Playing with chubby puppies is lots of fun for me.

I just love tacos to eat,

And sometimes chocolate for a treat.

Pink is a colour I like a lot,

My Skye puppy is the best present I ever got.

My favourite person is Robin, who is a gem,

So this, my first poem, is just for them!

Flynn Holborow (4)

Patacake Day Nursery, Cambridge

Ada's First Poem

My name is Ada and I go to preschool,

My best friend is India, who is really cool.

I watch CBeebies on TV,

Playing with magnets is lots of fun for me.

I just love roast chicken to eat,

And sometimes apple pie for a treat.

Purple is a colour I like a lot,

My apple pie is the best present I ever got.

My favourite person is India, who is a gem,

So this, my first poem, is just for them!

Ada Horsnel (4)

Patacake Day Nursery, Cambridge

Ezgi's First Poem

My name is Ezgi and I go to preschool,
My best friend is Alice, who is really cool.
I watch PAW Patrol on TV,
Playing with sand is lots of fun for me.
I just love bananas to eat,
And sometimes chocolate for a treat.
Purple and green are colours I like a lot,
My drum is the best present I ever got.
My favourite person is Ozan, who is a gem,
So this, my first poem, is just for them!

Ezgi Kaser (4)

Patacake Day Nursery, Cambridge

Finn's First Poem

My name is Finn and I go to preschool,
My best friend is Willow, who is really cool.
I watch PAW Patrol on TV,
Playing Octonauts is lots of fun for me.
I just love sausages to eat,
And sometimes chocolate cake for a treat.
Red is a colour I like a lot,
My Mini car is the best present I ever got.
My favourite person is Mummy, who is a gem,
So this, my first poem, is just for them!

Finn Baker-Cash (4)

Patacake Day Nursery, Cambridge

Maisy's First Poem

My name is Maisy and I go to preschool,

My best friend is Romilly, who is really cool.

I watch Minnie Mouse on TV,

Playing dressing up is lots of fun for me.

I just love pasta to eat,

And sometimes chocolate for a treat.

Pink is a colour I like a lot,

My Elsa toy is the best present I ever got.

My favourite person is Daddy, who is a gem,

So this, my first poem, is just for them!

Maisy Campbell (3)

Patacake Day Nursery, Cambridge

Samuel's First Poem

My name is Samuel and I go to preschool,

My best friend is Liam, who is really cool.

I watch Lightning McQueen on TV,

Playing cars is lots of fun for me.

I just love pasta to eat,

And sometimes sweets for a treat.

Blue is a colour I like a lot,

My fire car is the best present I ever got.

My favourite person is Daddy, who is a gem,

So this, my first poem, is just for them!

Samuel Ray (3)

Patacake Day Nursery, Cambridge

Amelia-Grace's First Poem

My name is Amelia-Grace and I go to preschool,

My best friends are Teddy and Tom, who are

really cool.

I watch Peppa Pig on TV,

Playing Barbie Cinderella is lots of fun for me.

I just love pasta and cheese to eat,

And sometimes Mummy's chocolate for a treat.

Yellow is a colour I like a lot,

My baby dolly is the best present I ever got.

My favourite people are Teddy and Lola, who are gems,

So this, my first poem, is just for them!

Amelia-Grace Godden (2)

Playtimes Preschool, Huntingdon

George's First Poem

My name is George and I go to preschool,

My best friends are Bradley and Freddie, who are really cool.

I watch PAW Patrol on TV,

Playing trains and dinosaurs is lots of fun for me.

I just love sausages to eat,

And sometimes Haribo for a treat.

Blue is a colour I like a lot,

My train set is the best present I ever got.

My favourite people are Mummy and Daddy, who are gems,

So this, my first poem, is just for them!

George Howell-Jones (2)

Playtimes Preschool, Huntingdon

Lily's First Poem

My name is Lily and I go to preschool,

My best friends are Isla and Rebel, who are really cool.

I watch PAW Patrol on TV,

Playing cycling is lots of fun for me.

I just love ham to eat,

And sometimes ice cream for a treat.

Pink is a colour I like a lot,

My Skye toy is the best present I ever got.

My favourite person is Mummy, who is a gem,

So this, my first poem, is just for them!

Lily Woods (3)

Playtimes Preschool, Huntingdon

Maisie's First Poem

My name is Maisie and I go to preschool,

My best friends are Isla and Toby, who are really cool.

I watch Tom and Jerry on TV,

Playing football is lots of fun for me.

I just love pizza to eat,

And sometimes lollipops for a treat.

Red is a colour I like a lot,

My doggy is the best present I ever got.

My favourite person is Jake, who is a gem,

So this, my first poem, is just for them!

Maisie Woods (3)

Playtimes Preschool, Huntingdon

Poppy's First Poem

My name is Poppy and I go to preschool,

My best friend is Mia, who is really cool.

I watch Peppa Pig on TV,

Playing with Lego is lots of fun for me.

I just love chicken nuggets and chips to eat,

And sometimes chocolate for a treat.

Pink is a colour I like a lot,

My pencils are the best present I've ever got.

My favourite person is Santa, who is a gem,

So this, my first poem, is just for them!

Poppy Watson (4)

Rainbow Bright Private Day Care, Ipswich

Kyle's First Poem

My name is Kyle and I go to preschool,
My best friend is Hugo, who is really cool.
I watch Tigers on TV,
Playing on Mum's phone is lots of fun for me.
I just love sausages to eat,
And sometimes ice cream and chocolate for
a treat.
Red is a colour I like a lot,
My tiger is the best present I ever got.
My favourite person is my big grandad, who is a gem,
So this, my first poem, is just for them!

Kyle Rogers (4)
Rainbow Bright Private Day Care, Ipswich

Isabel's First Poem

My name is Isabel and I go to preschool,

My best friend is Ava, who is really cool.

I watch Zootropolis on TV,

Playing dinosaurs is lots of fun for me.

I just love apples to eat,

And sometimes chocolate for a treat.

Purple is a colour I like a lot,

My PAW Patrol Look-out is the best present I

ever got.

My favourite person is Mummy, who is a gem,

So this, my first poem, is just for them!

Isabel Hatchard (3)

Rainbow Bright Private Day Care, Ipswich

Jasmine's First Poem

My name is Jasmine and I go to preschool,
My best friend is Alice, who is really cool.
I watch My Little Pony on TV,
Playing princesses is lots of fun for me.
I just love mash potato to eat,
And sometimes chocolate for a treat.
Purple is a colour I like a lot,
My Elsa dress is the best present I ever got.
My favourite person is Nana, who is a gem,
So this, my first poem, is just for them!

Jasmine Watson (4)
Rainbow Bright Private Day Care, Ipswich

Freya's First Poem

My name is Freya and I go to preschool,

My best friend is baby Evie, who is really cool.

I watch Barbie on TV,

Playing with puzzles is lots of fun for me.

I just love beans on toast to eat,

And sometimes sweets for a treat.

Pink is a colour I like a lot,

My Elsa and Anna are the best presents I ever got.

My favourite person is Mummy, who is a gem,

So this, my first poem, is just for them!

Freya Souter (3)

Rainbow Bright Private Day Care, Ipswich

Gracie's First Poem

My name is Gracie and I go to preschool,

My best friend is Suzie, who is really cool.

I watch Peppa Pig on TV,

Playing sleeping lions is lots of fun for me.

I just love rice to eat,

And sometimes chocolate for a treat.

Yellow is a colour I like a lot,

My chocolate coins are the best present I ever got.

My favourite person is Mummy, who is a gem,

So this, my first poem, is just for them!

Gracie Boyd (2)

Rainbow Bright Private Day Care, Ipswich

Suzie's First Poem

My name is Suzie and I go to preschool,

My best friend is Gracie, who is really cool.

I watch Frozen on TV,

Playing Nemo is lots of fun for me.

I just love pasta to eat,

And sometimes a lolly for a treat.

Purple is a colour I like a lot,

My Elsa is the best present I ever got.

My favourite person is Mummy and Daddy, who is

a gem,

So this, my first poem, is just for them!

Suzie White (2)

Rainbow Bright Private Day Care, Ipswich

Hugo's First Poem

My name is **Hugo** and I go to preschool,
My best friend is **Harris**, who is really cool.
I watch **PAW Patrol** on TV,
Playing **with Lego** is lots of fun for me.
I just love **sausages** to eat,
And sometimes **chocolate** for a treat.
Blue is a colour I like a lot,
My **Chase** is the best present I ever got.
My favourite person is **Daddy**, who is a gem,
So this, my first poem, is just for them!

Hugo French (3)
Rainbow Bright Private Day Care, Ipswich

Harris' First Poem

My name is **Harris** and I go to preschool,

My best friend is **Hugo**, who is really cool.

I watch **Flash** on TV,

Playing **turtles** is lots of fun for me.

I just love **sausages** to eat,

And sometimes **sweets** for a treat.

Red is a colour I like a lot,

My **Ninja Turtle** is the best present I ever got.

My favourite person is **Kyrell**, who is a gem,

So this, my first poem, is just for them!

Harris Scott (3)
Rainbow Bright Private Day Care, Ipswich

Alexis' First Poem

My name is Alexis and I go to preschool,

My best friend is Isaac (he is two), who is really cool.

I watch Hey Duggee, Ben & Holly and Mickey Mouse Club on TV,

Playing Doc McStuffins is lots of fun for me.

I just love sandwiches, hot dogs, bananas and apples to eat,

And sometimes an iced ginger man for a treat.

Pink and yellow are colours I like a lot,

My unicorn is the best present I ever got.

My favourite people are Mummy, Evie and Paul, who are gems,

So this, my first poem, is just for them!

Alexis Bloomfield (4)

Rosehill Playgroup, Ipswich

Jenna's First Poem

My name is Jenna and I go to preschool,

My best friends are Amina and Hope, who are

really cool.

I watch Peppa Pig and Peter Rabbit on TV,

Playing with Play-Doh is lots of fun for me.

I just love scones and breadsticks to eat,

And sometimes chocolate for a treat.

Pink and yellow are colours I like a lot,

My Sleeping Beauty pen is the best present I

ever got.

My favourite person is Mummy, who is a gem,

So this, my first poem, is just for them!

Jenna Foulkes (3)

Rosehill Playgroup, Ipswich

Holly's First Poem

My name is Holly and I go to preschool,

My best friend is Eden, who is really cool.

I watch Peppa Pig and Charley Bear on TV,

Playing bunnies, puzzles and bricks is lots of fun for me.

I just love strawberries, biscuits and spaghetti to eat,

And sometimes McDonald's for a treat.

Red is a colour I like a lot,

My kitten on a lead is the best present I ever got.

My favourite people are Mummy and my kitten, who are gems,

So this, my first poem, is just for them!

Holly Pearson (3)
Rosehill Playgroup, Ipswich

Saffire's First Poem

My name is Saffire and I go to preschool,

My best friends are Ana and Paula, who are

really cool.

I watch Elsa and Anna on TV,

Playing Barbie and princesses is lots of fun for me.

I just love potatoes to eat,

And sometimes sweeties for a treat.

Blue is a colour I like a lot,

My Barbie is the best present I ever got.

My favourite person is Mummy, who is a gem,

So this, my first poem, is just for them!

Saffire Marshall (4)

Rosehill Playgroup, Ipswich

Rosie's First Poem

My name is Rosie and I go to preschool,

My best friend is Hannah, who is really cool.

I watch Peppa Pig on TV,

Playing snakes and ladders is lots of fun for me.

I just love sweet orange pizza to eat,

And sometimes ice cream for a treat.

Red is a colour I like a lot,

My My Little Ponies are the best presents I ever got.

My favourite person is Hannah, who is a gem,

So this, my first poem, is just for them!

Rosie Adams (4)

Rosehill Playgroup, Ipswich

Jaycie-Lee's First Poem

My name is Jaycie-Lee and I go to preschool,

My best friend is Lexis, who is really cool.

I watch Dora and Peppa Pig on TV,

Playing daisy is lots of fun for me.

I just love chicken nuggets to eat,

And sometimes chocolate eggs for a treat.

Pink is a colour I like a lot,

My princess is the best present I ever got.

My favourite person is Mummy, who is a gem,

So this, my first poem, is just for them!

Jaycie-Lee Rose Rush (3)

Rosehill Playgroup, Ipswich

Ruby's First Poem

My name is Ruby and I go to preschool,

My best friend is Ethan, who is really cool.

I watch PAW Patrol on TV,

Playing dolls is lots of fun for me.

I just love jam sandwiches and yoghurt to eat,

And sometimes chocolate rolls for a treat.

Pink is a colour I like a lot,

My Barbies are the best present I ever got.

My favourite person is Ethan, who is a gem,

So this, my first poem, is just for them!

Ruby Bown (4)

Rosehill Playgroup, Ipswich

Charlie's First Poem

My name is Charlie and I go to preschool,
My best friend is Daddy, who is really cool.
I watch Peppa Pig on TV,
Playing cars and garages is lots of fun for me.
I just love snacks to eat,
And sometimes chocolate for a treat.
Green and blue are colours I like a lot,
My skateboard is the best present I ever got.
My favourite person is Daddy, who is a gem,
So this, my first poem, is just for them!

Charlie Hazell (3)

Rosehill Playgroup, Ipswich

Hannah's First Poem

My name is Hannah and I go to preschool,
My best friend is Rosie, who is really cool.
I watch Umizoomi on TV,
Playing babies is lots of fun for me.
I just love pancakes to eat,
And sometimes chocolate for a treat.
White and blue are colours I like a lot,
My Barbies are the best presents I ever got.
My favourite person is Owen, who is a gem,
So this, my first poem, is just for them!

Hannah Martina Walker (4)

Rosehill Playgroup, Ipswich

Lewis' First Poem

My name is Lewis and I go to preschool,

My best friend is Lewis, who is really cool.

I watch PAW Patrol on TV,

Playing cars is lots of fun for me.

I just love mushrooms to eat,

And sometimes sweeties for a treat.

Blue is a colour I like a lot,

My snowman is the best present I ever got.

My favourite people are Curtis and Mummy, who are gems,

So this, my first poem, is just for them!

Lewis Rosher (3)

Rosehill Playgroup, Ipswich

Sonny's First Poem

My name is Sonny and I go to preschool,

My best friend is Tyler, who is really cool.

I watch Power Rangers on TV,

Playing cars is lots of fun for me.

I just love Coco Pops to eat,

And sometimes a cake for a treat.

Blue is a colour I like a lot,

My orange monster truck is the best present I
ever got.

My favourite person is Mummy, who is a gem,

So this, my first poem, is just for them!

Sonny Webb (4)
Rosehill Playgroup, Ipswich

Blake's First Poem

My name is Blake and I go to preschool,

My best friend is Safwan, who is really cool.

I watch Marvels on TV,

Playing Iron Man is lots of fun for me.

I just love ham sandwiches to eat,

And sometimes sweets for a treat.

Brown is a colour I like a lot,

My Lion Guard is the best present I ever got.

My favourite person is Mummy, who is a gem,

So this, my first poem, is just for them!

Blake Creasey (4)

Rosehill Playgroup, Ipswich

Safwan's First Poem

My name is Safwan and I go to preschool,
My best friend is Blake, who is really cool.
I watch PAW Patrol on TV,
Playing cars is lots of fun for me.
I just love chocolate to eat,
And sometimes chocolate for a treat.
Red is a colour I like a lot,
My racing car is the best present I ever got.
My favourite person is Mum, who is a gem,
So this, my first poem, is just for them!

Safwan Bin Subhan-Miah (4)

Rosehill Playgroup, Ipswich

Violet's First Poem

My name is Violet and I go to preschool,

My best friend is Ivy, who is really cool.

I watch Tangled on TV,

Playing dolls is lots of fun for me.

I just love pizza to eat,

And sometimes lollipops for a treat.

Pink is a colour I like a lot,

My scarf is the best present I ever got.

My favourite person is Mummy, who is a gem,

So this, my first poem, is just for them!

Violet Jean Richardson (3)

Rosehill Playgroup, Ipswich

Lily-May's First Poem

My name is **Lily-May** and I go to preschool,

My best friend is **Casey Bailey**, who is really cool.

I watch **Peter Rabbit, Ben & Holly and Peppa Pig** on TV,

Playing **with dolls** is lots of fun for me.

I just love **pasta and roast dinners** to eat,

And sometimes **sweeties** for a treat.

Pink is a colour I like a lot,

My **bike** is the best present I ever got.

My favourite people are **Mummy and Daddy**, who are gems,

So this, my first poem, is just for them!

Lily-May Bell (4)

Stepping Stones Preschool, Newmarket

Dexter's First Poem

My name is Dexter and I go to preschool,

My best friend is Thomas, who is really cool.

I watch nursery rhymes on TV,

Playing with cars is lots of fun for me.

I just love macaroni cheese to eat,

And sometimes a Smarties ice cream for a treat.

Blue is a colour I like a lot,

My Lego is the best present I ever got.

My favourite person is Albert, my cousin, who is

a gem,

So this, my first poem, is just for them!

Dexter Pidsley-Cook (3)

Stepping Stones Preschool, Newmarket

Dougie's First Poem

My name is Dougie and I go to preschool,

My best friend is Aiden, who is really cool.

I watch Road Rangers on TV,

Playing with trains and toys is lots of fun for me.

I just love sausages and dip dip to eat,

And sometimes wiggly worms for a treat.

Green is a colour I like a lot,

My big train track is the best present I ever got.

My favourite person is Mummy, who is a gem,

So this, my first poem, is just for them!

Dougie Bear Mclean (2)

Stepping Stones Preschool, Newmarket

Jacob's First Poem

My name is Jacob and I go to preschool,

My best friend is Taiyo, who is really cool.

I watch Blaze and the Monster Machines
on TV,

Playing Thunderbirds is lots of fun for me.

I just love pizza to eat,

And sometimes sweeties for a treat.

Blue is a colour I like a lot,

My Thunderbird toy is the best present I ever got.

My favourite person is Taiyo, who is a gem,

So this, my first poem, is just for them!

Jacob Kirby (4)
Stepping Stones Preschool, Newmarket

Kodi's First Poem

My name is Kodi and I go to preschool,

My best friend is Ellis, who is really cool.

I watch Thomas on TV,

Playing trains and animals is lots of fun for me.

I just love chicken nuggets to eat,

And sometimes strawberry ice cream for a treat.

Blue is a colour I like a lot,

My Tidmouth shed is the best present I ever got.

My favourite person is Mummy, who is a gem,

So this, my first poem, is just for them!

Kodi Lockwood (3)

Stepping Stones Preschool, Newmarket

Ellis' First Poem

My name is Ellis and I go to preschool,

My best friend is Taiyo, who is really cool.

I watch Blaze and the Monster Machines
on TV,

Playing with toy buses is lots of fun for me.

I just love pasta to eat,

And sometimes sweeties for a treat.

Purple is a colour I like a lot,

My bike is the best present I ever got.

My favourite person is Mummy, who is a gem,

So this, my first poem, is just for them!

Ellis Jeffery (3)
Stepping Stones Preschool, Newmarket

Ryan's First Poem

My name is Ryan and I go to preschool,

My best friend is Ben, who is really cool.

I watch SpondgeBob SquarePants on TV,

Playing Xbox is lots of fun for me.

I just love pork chops to eat,

And sometimes chocolate for a treat.

Red is a colour I like a lot,

My Mario Cart race track is the best present I

ever got.

My favourite person is Mummy, who is a gem,

So this, my first poem, is just for them!

Ryan William Brewer (4)

Stepping Stones Preschool, Newmarket

Annabella's First Poem

My name is Annabella and I go to preschool,

My best friend is Sophia, who is really cool.

I watch Masha and the Bear on TV,

Playing hide and seek is lots of fun for me.

I just love apples and grapes to eat,

And sometimes an ice pop for a treat.

Pink is a colour I like a lot,

My bike is the best present I ever got.

My favourite person is Daddy, who is a gem,

So this, my first poem, is just for them!

Annabella Marie Rodman (3)

Stepping Stones Preschool, Newmarket

Drayton's First Poem

My name is Drayton and I go to preschool,

My best friend is Thurloe, who is really cool.

I watch PAW Patrol on TV,

Playing Ninja Turtles is lots of fun for me.

I just love pasta to eat,

And sometimes chocolate for a treat.

Blue is a colour I like a lot,

My cardboard pirate ship is the best present I ever got.

My favourite person is me, I'm a gem,

So this, my first poem, is just for them!

Drayton Hayes (2)

Stepping Stones Preschool, Newmarket

Thurloe's First Poem

My name is Thurloe and I go to preschool,

My best friend is Jacob, who is really cool.

I watch Jungle Book on TV,

Playing Ninja Turtles is lots of fun for me.

I just love chicken to eat,

And sometimes watermelon for a treat.

Dark blue is a colour I like a lot,

My jelly maker is the best present I ever got.

My favourite person is Minky, who is a gem,

So this, my first poem, is just for them!

Thurloe Hayes (4)

Stepping Stones Preschool, Newmarket

Ben's First Poem

My name is Ben and I go to preschool,

My best friend is Mama, who is really cool.

I watch Counting Stars on TV,

Playing with cars is lots of fun for me.

I just love cucumber to eat,

And sometimes ice lollies for a treat.

Bright blue is a colour I like a lot,

My monster truck is the best present I ever got.

My favourite person is Daddy, who is a gem,

So this, my first poem, is just for them!

Ben Shevki (4)

Stepping Stones Preschool, Newmarket

Henry's First Poem

My name is Henry and I go to preschool,

My best friend is Grandad Carl, who is really cool.

I watch Chuggingtons on TV,

Playing hide-and-seek is lots of fun for me.

I just love fruit to eat,

And sometimes chocolate for a treat.

Red is a colour I like a lot,

My bus bed is the best present I ever got.

My favourite person is Nanny Sally, who is a gem,

So this, my first poem, is just for them!

Henry Thomas Palmer (2)

Stepping Stones Preschool, Newmarket

Rosie's First Poem

My name is Rosie and I go to preschool,

My best friend is Jacob, who is really cool.

I watch PAW Patrol on TV,

Playing babies is lots of fun for me.

I just love prawn crackers to eat,

And sometimes choccy for a treat.

Purple is a colour I like a lot,

My car-set baby is the best present I ever got.

My favourite person is Maria, who is a gem,

So this, my first poem, is just for them!

Rosie O'Brien (3)

Stepping Stones Preschool, Newmarket

Florrie's First Poem

My name is Florrie and I go to preschool,

My best friend is Hugo, who is really cool.

I watch Frozen on TV,

Playing with Play-Doh is lots of fun for me.

I just love pasta to eat,

And sometimes Kinder Eggs for a treat.

Yellow is a colour I like a lot,

My scooter is the best present I ever got.

My favourite person is Mummy, who is a gem,

So this, my first poem, is just for them!

Florrie Shaw (3)
Stepping Stones Preschool, Newmarket

Iyla's First Poem

My name is Iyla and I go to preschool,

My best friend is Daisy, who is really cool.

I watch Trolls on TV,

Playing dolls is lots of fun for me.

I just love rice to eat,

And sometimes chocolate eggs for a treat.

Lilac is a colour I like a lot,

My Barbie is the best present I ever got.

My favourite person is Mummy, who is a gem,

So this, my first poem, is just for them!

Iyla Frankie Jack (3)
Stepping Stones Preschool, Newmarket

Rowan's First Poem

My name is Rowan and I go to preschool,

My best friend is Noah, who is really cool.

I watch PAW Patrol on TV,

Playing bin lorries is lots of fun for me.

I just love banana to eat,

And sometimes chocolate for a treat.

Pink is a colour I like a lot,

My mixer and brush are the best presents I ever got.

My favourite people are Mummy and Daddy, who are gems,

So this, my first poem, is just for them!

Rowan Kearney (4)

Sunflower Nursery, Cambridge

Linus' First Poem

My name is Linus and I go to preschool,

My best friends are everbody, they are really cool.

I watch PAW Patrol on TV,

Playing trains is lots of fun for me.

I just love sweetcorn to eat,

And sometimes a lolly for a treat.

Pink and purple are colours I like a lot,

My Lego is the best present I ever got.

My favourite person is Daddy, who is a gem,

So this, my first poem, is just for them!

Lingwen Linus Chin (4)

Sunflower Nursery, Cambridge

Thom's First Poem

My name is Thom and I go to preschool,

My best friend is Henry, who is really cool.

I watch Transformers on TV,

Playing Transformers is lots of fun for me.

I just love hummus and ham wraps to eat,

And sometimes jelly tots for a treat.

Indigo and violet are colours I like a lot,

My massive Transformer is the best present I

ever got.

My favourite person is Iris, who is a gem,

So this, my first poem, is just for them!

Thom Blanchard (4)
Sunflower Nursery, Cambridge

Leila's First Poem

My name is Leila and I go to preschool,

My best friend is Rosie, who is really cool.

I watch Frozen on TV,

Playing with my rainbow hairband is lots of fun
for me.

I just love sausages to eat,

And sometimes a lolly for a treat.

Pink is a colour I like a lot,

My nice teddy is the best present I ever got.

My favourite people are all my family, who are gems,

So this, my first poem, is just for them!

Leila Daisy Fievet (3)

Sunflower Nursery, Cambridge

Henry's First Poem

My name is Henry and I go to preschool,
My best friend is Thom, who is really cool.
I watch Transformers on TV,
Playing bits and bobs is lots of fun for me.
I just love fish and chips to eat,
And sometimes chocolate ice cream for a treat.
Blue is a colour I like a lot,
My Transformer is the best present I ever got.
My favourite person is Isabella, who is a gem,
So this, my first poem, is just for them!

Henry Heywood (4)
Sunflower Nursery, Cambridge

Margaret's First Poem

My name is Margaret and I go to preschool,

My best friend is Grace, who is really cool.

I watch My Little Pony on TV,

Playing puppies and mummies is lots of fun for me.

I just love fish and chips to eat,

And sometimes an orange for a treat.

Pink is a colour I like a lot,

My polar bear is the best present I ever got.

My favourite person is Emily, who is a gem,

So this, my first poem, is just for them!

Margaret Zi Yin Li (3)

Sunflower Nursery, Cambridge

Maria's First Poem

My name is **Maria** and I go to preschool,

My best friend is **Georgie**, who is really cool.

I watch **Frozen** on TV,

Playing **with trains** is lots of fun for me.

I just love **peas and potatoes** to eat,

And sometimes **cake** for a treat.

Pink is a colour I like a lot,

My **fluffy, pink unicorn** is the best present I ever got.

My favourite person is **Ana, my sister**, who is a gem,

So this, my first poem, is just for them!

Maria Popescu (4)
Sunflower Nursery, Cambridge

Georgie's First Poem

My name is Georgie and I go to preschool,

My best friend is Lola, who is really cool.

I watch PAW Patrol on TV,

Playing with my Rainbow Dash toy is lots of fun for me.

I just love peas and carrots to eat,

And sometimes cake for a treat.

Pink is a colour I like a lot,

My Rainbow Dash is the best present I ever got.

My favourite person is Daddy, who is a gem,

So this, my first poem, is just for them!

Georgie-Rose Jeffrey (3)
Sunflower Nursery, Cambridge

Nicholas' First Poem

My name is Nicholas and I go to preschool,

My best friend is Lily, who is really cool.

I watch Peppa Pig on TV,

Playing car and garages is lots of fun for me.

I just love carrots to eat,

And sometimes biscuits for a treat.

Blue is a colour I like a lot,

My blue bear and blue cat are the best presents I

ever got.

My favourite person is Lily, who is a gem,

So this, my first poem, is just for them!

Nicholas Jameson (3)

Sunflower Nursery, Cambridge

Beatrice's First Poem

My name is **Beatrice** and I go to preschool,

My best friend is **Alicia**, who is really cool.

I watch **Peter Rabbit** on TV,

Playing **doctors** is lots of fun for me.

I just love **spaghetti** to eat,

And sometimes **ice cream** for a treat.

Yellow is a colour I like a lot,

My **bicycle** is the best present I ever got.

My favourite person is **my daddy, Tim**, who is a gem,

So this, my first poem, is just for them!

Beatrice Raine (4)

Sunflower Nursery, Cambridge

Kate's First Poem

My name is Kate and I go to preschool,
My best friend is Henri, who is really cool.
I watch PAW Patrol on TV,
Playing Playmobil is lots of fun for me.
I just love macaroni cheese to eat,
And sometimes ice cream for a treat.
Pink is a colour I like a lot,
My scooter is the best present I ever got.
My favourite person is Mummy, who is a gem,
So this, my first poem, is just for them!

Kate Bleazard (4)

Sunflower Nursery, Cambridge

Jasper's First Poem

My name is Jasper and I go to preschool,

My best friend is Ivan, who is really cool.

I watch Power Rangers on TV,

Playing with Lego is lots of fun for me.

I just love blue eggs to eat,

And sometimes sweets for a treat.

Blue is a colour I like a lot,

My Blaze the car is the best present I ever got.

My favourite person is Billy, who is a gem,

So this, my first poem, is just for them!

Jasper Giles (4)

Sunflower Nursery, Cambridge

Lawrence's First Poem

My name is Lawrence and I go to preschool,

My best friend is Thom, who is really cool.

I watch Lion Guard on TV,

Playing Transformers is lots of fun for me.

I just love chicken to eat,

And sometimes watermelon for a treat.

Blue is a colour I like a lot,

My kung fu is the best present I ever got.

My favourite person is Henry, who is a gem,

So this, my first poem, is just for them!

Lawrence Heywood (4)

Sunflower Nursery, Cambridge

Ivan's First Poem

My name is Ivan and I go to preschool,

My best friend is Jasper, who is really cool.

I watch Spider-Man on TV,

Playing the letter game is lots of fun for me.

I just love porridge to eat,

And sometimes a biscuit for a treat.

White is a colour I like a lot,

My iPad is the best present I ever got.

My favourite person is Mummy, who is a gem,

So this, my first poem, is just for them!

Ivan Kolesnik (4)

Sunflower Nursery, Cambridge

Kasey's First Poem

My name is Kasey and I go to preschool,

My best friend is Sara, who is really cool.

I watch CBeebies on TV,

Playing hairdressers is lots of fun for me.

I just love rice to eat,

And sometimes sweeties for a treat.

Pink is a colour I like a lot,

My toy baby is the best present I ever got.

My favourite person is my brother, who is a gem,

So this, my first poem, is just for them!

Kasey Kwateng (4)

Sunflower Nursery, Cambridge

Rosie-May's First Poem

My name is Rosie-May and I go to preschool,

My best friend is Ava, who is really cool.

I watch Peppa Pig on TV,

Playing with Daddy is lots of fun for me.

I just love pasta to eat,

And sometimes chocolate for a treat.

Blue is a colour I like a lot,

My bike is the best present I ever got.

My favourite person is Daddy, who is a gem,

So this, my first poem, is just for them!

Rosie-May Anne Abbs (4)

Sunflower Nursery, Cambridge

Holly's First Poem

My name is Holly and I go to preschool,

My best friend is Leila, who is really cool.

I watch Peppa Pig on TV,

Playing babies is lots of fun for me.

I just love noodles to eat,

And sometimes lollipops for a treat.

Purple is a colour I like a lot,

My unicorn is the best present I ever got.

My favourite person is Alex, who is a gem,

So this, my first poem, is just for them!

Holly York (4)

Sunflower Nursery, Cambridge

103

Anamaya's First Poem

My name is Anamaya and I go to preschool,

My best friend is Kasey, who is really cool.

I watch Frozen on TV,

Drawing is lots of fun for me.

I just love beans to eat,

And sometimes oranges for a treat.

Pink is a colour I like a lot,

My grey cat is the best present I ever got.

My favourite person is Leila, who is a gem,

So this, my first poem, is just for them!

Anamaya Rose Kumar (3)

Sunflower Nursery, Cambridge

Erin's First Poem

My name is Erin and I go to preschool,

My best friend is Emily, who is really cool.

I watch Trolls, the film on TV,

Playing with my babies is lots of fun for me.

I just love cheesy pasta to eat,

And sometimes chocolate digger biscuits for

a treat.

Pink is a colour I like a lot,

My wooden doll's house is the best present I

ever got.

My favourite person is Mummy, who is a gem,

So this, my first poem, is just for them!

Erin Howes (2)

Trinity Nursery, Lowestoft

Brody's First Poem

My name is Brody and I go to preschool,

My best friends are Ethan, Erin and Jack, who
are really cool.

I watch Batman on TV,

Playing cars and racing around is lots of fun
for me.

I just love hot dogs to eat,

And sometimes chocolate for a treat.

Red, blue, pink, orange and purple are colours
I like a lot,

My Batman car is the best present I ever got.

My favourite person is Mummy, who is a gem,

So this, my first poem, is just for them!

Brody Baxter (3)

Trinity Nursery, Lowestoft

Emily's First Poem

My name is Emily and I go to preschool,

My best friend is Ivy, who is really cool.

I watch Peppa Pig and Frolls (Trolls) on TV,

Playing crocodiles is lots of fun for me.

I just love sandwiches to eat,

And sometimes sweeties for a treat.

Green, purple and pink are colours I like a lot,

My Frolls (Trolls) bracelet is the best present I

ever got.

My favourite person is Daddy, who is a gem,

So this, my first poem, is just for them!

Emily Pearl Newton (3)

Trinity Nursery, Lowestoft

Mia-Rose's First Poem

My name is Mia-Rose and I go to preschool,

My best friends are Archie, Ivy and Maisie, who are really cool.

I watch PAW Patrol and Ben & Holly on TV,

Playing on my bike is lots of fun for me.

I just love pizza to eat,

And sometimes chocolate for a treat.

Pink is a colour I like a lot,

My Elsa doll is the best present I ever got.

My favourite person is Mummy, who is a gem,

So this, my first poem, is just for them!

Mia-Rose Woodard (4)

Trinity Nursery, Lowestoft

Archie's First Poem

My name is Archie and I go to preschool,

My best friend is Mia, who is really cool.

I watch PAW Patrol on TV,

Playing PAW Patrol is lots of fun for me.

I just love spaghetti Bolognese to eat,

And sometimes ice cream for a treat.

Red is a colour I like a lot,

My PAW Patrol Aqua Doodle is the best present I

ever got.

My favourite people are Daddy, Mummy, Nanny

and Grandad, who are gems,

So this, my first poem, is just for them!

Archie Theobald (3)

Trinity Nursery, Lowestoft

Ivy's First Poem

My name is Ivy and I go to preschool,

My best friend is Summer, who is really cool.

I watch Barbie: Life in the Dream House on TV,

Playing with Barbies is lots of fun for me.

I just love pineapple to eat,

And sometimes sweets for a treat.

Pink is a colour I like a lot,

My Barbie Dream House is the best present I

ever got.

My favourite person is Mummy, who is a gem,

So this, my first poem, is just for them!

Ivy Grace Harrison (3)

Trinity Nursery, Lowestoft

Ethan's First Poem

My name is Ethan and I go to preschool,

My best friend is Brody, who is really cool.

I watch Scooby-Doo on TV,

Playing with my toy cars is lots of fun for me.

I just love chicken tikka masala to eat,

And sometimes ice cream for a treat.

Green is a colour I like a lot,

My remote control car is the best present I

ever got.

My favourite person is Daddy, who is a gem,

So this, my first poem, is just for them!

Ethan Howes (3)

Trinity Nursery, Lowestoft

Jack's First Poem

My name is Jack and I go to preschool,

My best friend is Emily, who is really cool.

I watch Thomas the Tank on TV,

Playing trains and cars is lots of fun for me.

I just love cheese to eat,

And sometimes chocolate fingers for a treat.

Blue is a colour I like a lot,

My train table is the best present I ever got.

My favourite person is Hehe (Daizee), who is a gem,

So this, my first poem, is just for them!

Jack Graham (3)

Trinity Nursery, Lowestoft

Christopher-Junior's First Poem

My name is Christopher-Junior and I go to preschool,
My best friend is Destiny, who is really cool.
I watch birdies on TV,
Playing Thomas is lots of fun for me.
I just love cake and biscuits to eat,
And sometimes I go to the park for a treat.
Green is a colour I like a lot,
My train is the best present I ever got.
My favourite person is Daddy, who is a gem,
So this, my first poem, is just for them!

Christopher-Junior Jayden Spencer (3)
Trinity Nursery, Lowestoft

Enid's First Poem

My name is Enid and I go to preschool,

My best friend is Callum, who is really cool.

I watch PJ Masks on TV,

Playing hide-and-seek is lots of fun for me.

I just love cucumber to eat,

And sometimes Smarties for a treat.

Blue is a colour I like a lot,

My Hungry Hippo game is the best present I

ever got.

My favourite person is Billy, who is a gem,

So this, my first poem, is just for them!

Enid Frederick (3)

Trinity Nursery, Lowestoft

My First Poem

We hope you have enjoyed reading this book – and that you will continue to enjoy it in the coming years.

If you're a young writer who enjoys reading and creative writing, or the parent of an enthusiastic poet or story writer, do visit our websites, www.myfirstpoem.com and www.youngwriters.co.uk. Here you will find free competitions, workshops and games, as well as recommended reads, a poetry glossary and our blog.

If you would like to order further copies of this book, or any of our other titles, then please give us a call or visit www.myfirstpoem.com.

My First Poem
Remus House
Coltsfoot Drive
Peterborough
PE2 9BF

Tel: 01733 898110
info@myfirstpoem.com